PIANO SOLO

OUTLAND

THE SERIES

USIC FROM THE ORIGINAL TELEVISION SOUNDTRACK

ISBN 978-1-5400-1423-8

HAL•LEONARD®

Visit Hal Leonard Online at
www.halleonard.com

Contact Us:
Hal Leonard
7777 West Bluemound Road
Milwaukee, WI 53213
Email: info@halleonard.com

In Europe contact:
Hal Leonard Europe Limited
42 Wigmore Street
Marylebone, London, W1U 2RN
Email: info@halleonardeurope.com

In Australia contact:
Hal Leonard Australia Pty. Ltd.
4 Lentara Court
Cheltenham, Victoria, 3192 Australia
Email: info@halleonard.com.au

CONTENTS

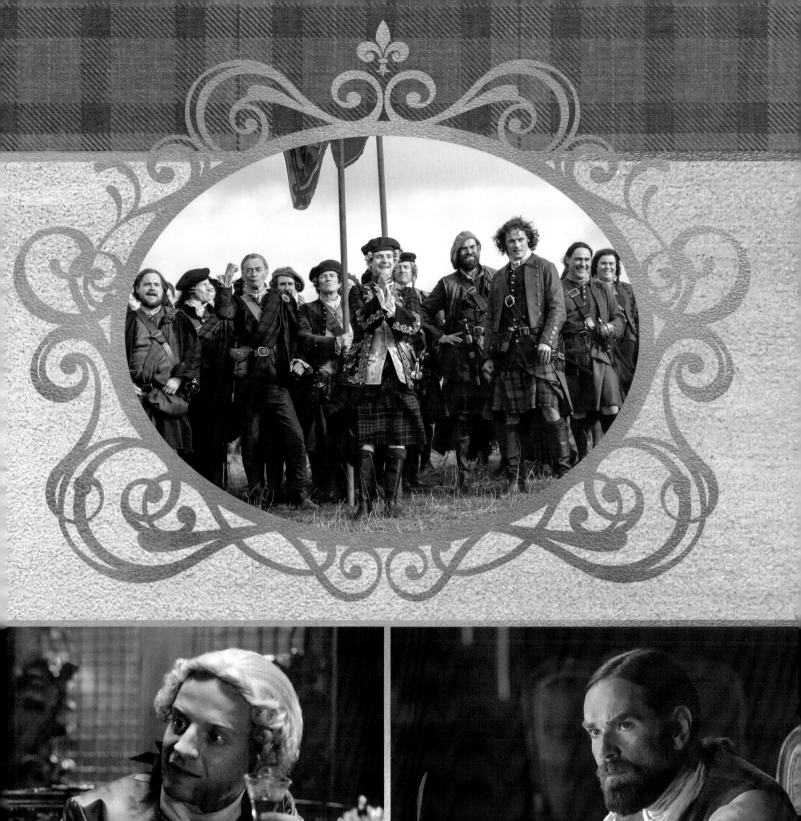

THE SKYE BOAT SONG

Traditional Music
Lyrics by ROBERT LOUIS STEVENSON
Arranged by BEAR McCREARY

Moderately slow, with a lilt

Sing me a song of a lass that is gone. Say, could that

lass be I? Mer - ry of soul, she sailed on a

day, o - ver the sea to Skye. Bil - low and

breeze, is - lands and seas, moun - tains of rain and sun,

CLAIRE AND JAMIE THEME

By BEAR McCREARY

COMIN' THRO' THE RYE

Traditional
Arranged by BEAR McCREARY

FAITH

By BEAR McCREARY

Slowly

FRANK THEME
(A Car Accident)

By BEAR McCREARY

LEAVE THE PAST BEHIND

By BEAR McCREARY

JOHN GREY

By BEAR McCREARY

MRS. FITZ

By BEAR McCREARY

DANCE OF THE DRUIDS

Traditional Lyrics
Music by BEAR McCREARY

MOCH SA MHADAINN

Traditional Music
Arranged by BEAR McCREARY

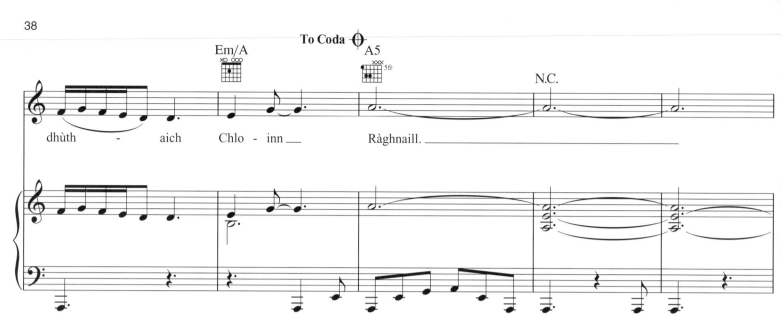

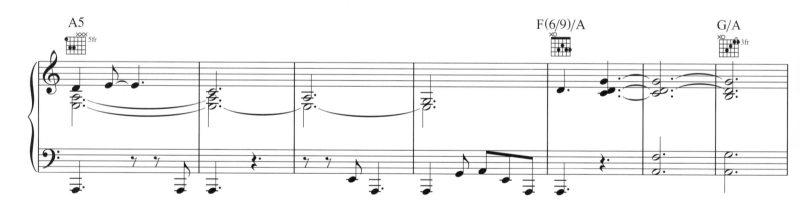

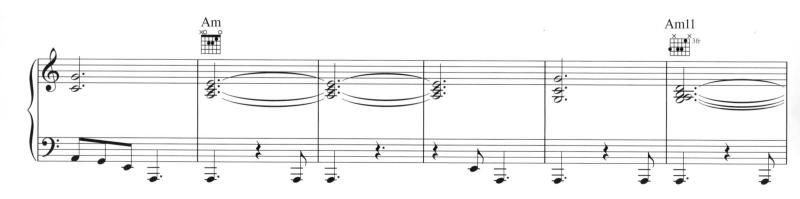

PEOPLE DISAPPEAR ALL THE TIME

By BEAR McCREARY

THE SKYE BOAT SONG
(Extended)

Traditional Music
Lyrics by ROBERT LOUIS STEVENSON
Arranged by BEAR McCREARY

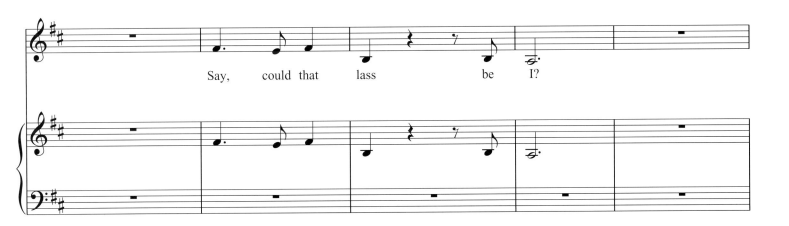

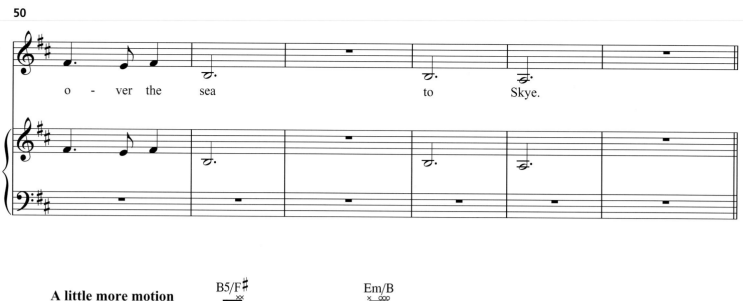

o - ver the sea to Skye.

A little more motion

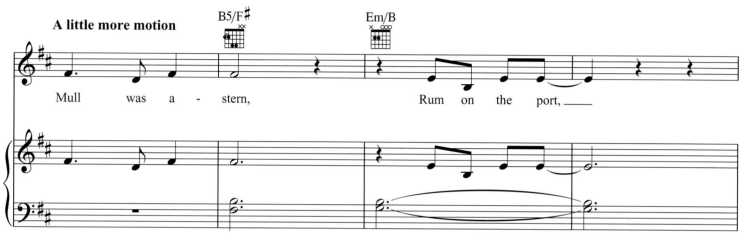

Mull was a - stern, Rum on the port, ___

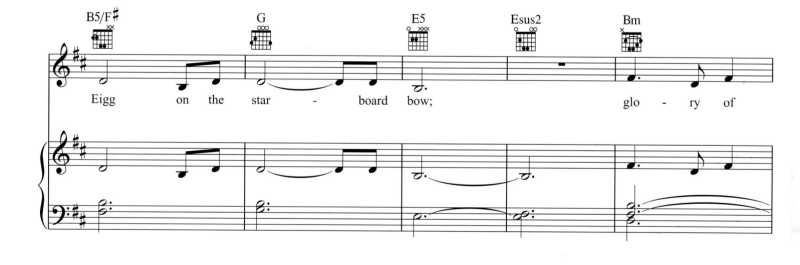

Eigg on the star - board bow; glo - ry of

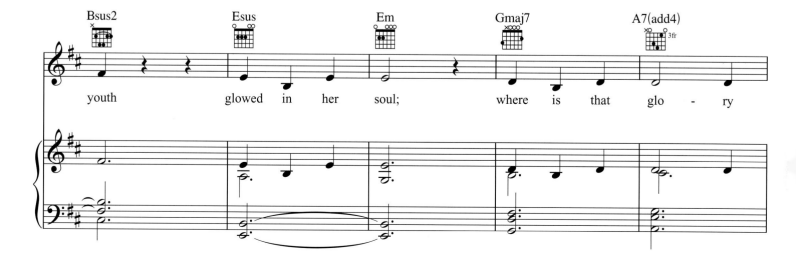

youth glowed in her soul; where is that glo - ry